From the Heart

DAVE MILLER

First hardcover edition November 2020
ISBN 978-1-7336287-8-5
Polar Sky Publishing LLC

TABLE OF CONTENTS

The art of cooking has always been fascinating to me. It's more than just a daily chore. I've often viewed it as an opportunity to create and express. Even if the finished product isn't as glamorous as you may have hoped, the effort and the passion cannot be denied.

Cooking is very similar to being in a relationship; what you put in, is what you get out. Giving 50% effort will never be enough. 100% is always necessary.

The irony of cooking is that two individuals can use the same exact recipe, simmer overtop of the same low flame and cook for exactly the same length of time and still manage to get different results. The reality is, if it's not from the heart, the cooking process will not matter, and the finished product will reflect that.

Welcome to From The Heart

Spicy Spinach Dip

1 pack of Lipton Vegetable Soup Mix

10 ounces sour cream

10 ounces chopped spinach (frozen)

Sriracha sauce

Prep: 10 minutes

Cook: 7 minutes

Total: 17 minutes

Servings: 4

In a mixing bowl, combine your Lipton Veggie Soup Mix with 10 ounces of sour cream. Mix and set aside. I found it easier to use the frozen spinach because it was already chopped, and it cooks rather quickly. Follow the directions on the packaging to prepare the spinach. It can either be microwaved or made on the stovetop; I was rather hungry at the time so I nuked (microwaved) mine.

Once your spinach is cooked, you'll want to drain all of the water. Add a few spoonfuls of spinach at a time to your sour cream mixture and stir. Repeat this process until all of the spinach is mixed in.

Then, add about five or six squirts of Sriracha sauce for the perfect amount of spice, and stir. Finally, put the dip in the fridge for an hour or two. When it's chilled, spread it on your favorite slice of bread, dip your favorite veggies in it or just have it with a few crackers. It's delicious. I hope you guys enjoy!

Tuna, tuna, tuna.....my how I love tuna! If I could eat it everyday, I definitely would. When I learned that you could use avocado as a mayo substitute in tuna, I was elated. The first time I made it, it came out ridiculously wrong because I didn't know how to pick an avocado. The result was more so avocado chunks and tuna, which was not the goal.

When picking your avocado for your tuna, especially if you want to eat it the day of, make sure that the avocado is soft before you buy it. This small, yet important, detail makes it substantially easier to mix the avocado with the tuna. This recipe is super easy and it plates well for when you're having guests over.

Avocado Tuna

1 avocado

8 ounce can of tuna in water

1/4 teaspoon Himalayan salt

1/4 teaspoon black pepper

1/4 cup diced red onions

1/4 cup diced red peppers

Prep: 10 minutes

Servings: 2

The first thing you'll want to do is cut your avocado in half. Do this carefully so you don't ruin the skin because you're going to place your tuna in it when you're done. Cut the avocado in half from top to bottom. When cutting, you can use the core on the inside as placement to make sure your cut is even. Once the avocado is cut, slightly twist each half in opposite directions so they can detach from one another.

For this next step, I found it easier to use a tablespoon to scoop out the core (the brown ball in the middle) and throw it in the trash. Now you can scoop the avocado out from both halves and put it into a small mixing bowl. Being as though you picked the right avocado you can use your spoon and mash it on the inside of the bowl.

Open your can of tuna and drain the water out. Then add the tuna to the avocado; you can also add your onions and peppers in as well. Once everything is added, mix it all up and add your salt and pepper. I prefer my tuna cold so I recommend refrigerating before serving it, but when you're ready to serve it just scoop it out and put it back in the avocado skin and you'll have a lite, attractive and tasty snack. Spread it on some crackers or eat it with a fork right out of the avocado skin. I hope you guys enjoy.

This dish has become one of my favorites. I've made broccoli tots in the past, but they were only okay. I felt they needed something extra. Then, the light bulb went off and I decided to use cranberries. Dried cranberries were the perfect ingredient to give this healthy snack the extra pop that it needed.

One thing that I've learned along my cooking journey is that fresh veggies are always the best way to go. Of course, they are better for your insides, but they also tend to taste better, and you'll feel better knowing that you're putting the absolute best foods in your body.

Broccoli Tots

1 tablespoon coconut (or olive) oil

3 cups fresh broccoli florets

1 cup dried cranberries

1 teaspoon garlic powder

1/2 cup panko bread crumbs

1/4 cup seasoned bread crumbs

1/2 teaspoon baking powder

3 large eggs

Prep: 15 minutes

Cook: 25 minutes

Total: 40 minutes

Servings: 4

This recipe is fairly easy. The first two things you should do is coat the pan with one tablespoon of coconut (or olive) oil and preheat your oven to 400 degrees. Now it's time to mix!

Break the florets off the main stalk of broccoli and cut the smaller stalks off as well. Using a sharp knife, cut the florets into small pieces. Once you cut three cups worth, pour them in your mixing bowl. In the same mixing bowl, add your cranberries, garlic powder, panko and seasoned bread crumbs. Mix well.

In a separate bowl, crack your three eggs and beat them. Pour the beaten eggs over all the ingredients in your mixing bowl and stir everything together.

Next, you'll want to grease your baking sheet. Olive oil has always been my go to, but as of lately I've been using coconut oil. Both work equally as good. This next part is the most tedious part, but once you're done, it will be worth the work.

Take about a healthy teaspoon worth of your mixture and begin to form your tots. Place them on your baking sheet and put those bad boys in the oven and let your oven do what it does. In about 20 minutes your tots will have a slight brown on them and will be ready to serve.

Bonus Recipe

This is my all purpose "Spicy Dipping Sauce." I used two soft avocados, vegan mayo, sriracha sauce and paprika. Using a knife, cut around the middle of the avocado until you have two halves. Remove the core and use a spoon to scoop out the avocado to remove it from the skin and put it in a small mixing bowl. Mash the avocados until there are no chunks, add a tablespoon of vegan mayonnaise. Last, but certainly not least, put a few squirts of sriracha sauce or if your tongue can stand the heat add a few more and few dashes of paprika. Mix it all together and you'll have the perfect Spicy Dipping Sauce that can be used for almost any food on your choice.

If my memory serves me correctly, I believe that I really changed my diet in 2014. At the time, I wasn't overweight; however, I was out of shape and I knew that changing my diet was the move for a few different reasons, age being one of them. Being 32 (which isn't old at all), I just knew that if I tackled my eating routine and habits that I could get a jump start on my health. As much as we all know the effects that working out has in our bodies, eating well is and will always be the key factor.

The interesting thing about me wanting to change my diet is that unconsciously I forgot what was instilled in me by my father. I remember being in elementary school and going to visit my dad on weekends. I would be utterly disappointed in the options available for me to eat. As a child, of course I didn't take it as him eating well.

It was strange because I was used to craving certain things, things that he would not have, so that is when I learned how to adapt. I vividly remember having turkey bacon for the first time at my dad's house, because he didn't eat pork products. It was a new thing to me, and even though I was used to eating pork bacon, turkey bacon had a

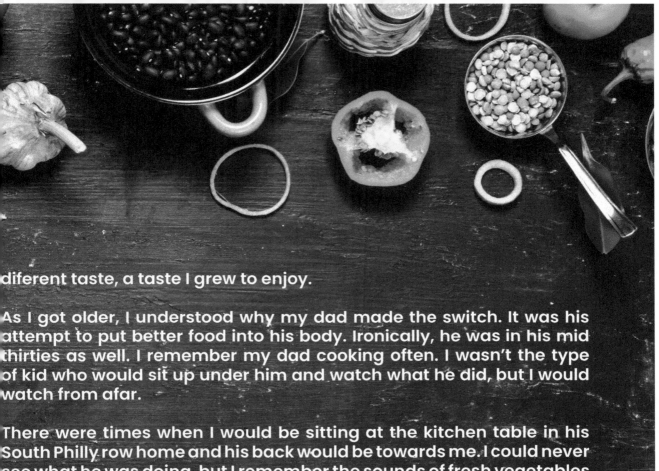

diferent taste, a taste I grew to enjoy.

As I got older, I understood why my dad made the switch. It was his attempt to put better food into his body. Ironically, he was in his mid thirties as well. I remember my dad cooking often. I wasn't the type of kid who would sit up under him and watch what he did, but I would watch from afar.

There were times when I would be sitting at the kitchen table in his South Philly row home and his back would be towards me. I could never see what he was doing, but I remember the sounds of fresh vegetables snapping and the knife hitting the cutting board after every slice. Then, after detailed and precise preparation, I would start to smell an aroma. Often, it was something I had never smelled, and a taste I had never been introduced to, however, the flavor was undeniably good, different, but definitely good.

Pop, I've taken more things from you than you would probably ever know, and for that, I thank you and I Love you.

They don't call it America's favorite food for nothing. Pizza is the one food that most people love to eat. It's pretty much the one thing that's hard to mess up if you know what you're doing. Some of my favorite childhood moments involve pizza.

I remember being a kid and during the summer months my cousins and I pretty much lived at the swimming pool. We would swim the days away. The pool opened at 1pm and we were there at 12:45pm waiting in line. After swimming for 4 hours, there was nothing better than a slice of pepperoni pizza from Papp's Pizza.

As we grew older and started to watch what we ate, I realized that the part of the pizza we loved the most is the part that is probably the worst for us, the crust. Once I discovered cauliflower crust, my life changed forever. Here you'll find a quick recipe for homemade crust; however, you can purchase one already made at your local grocery store.

Cauliflower Crust Pizza Pie

2 1/2 tablespoons pizza sauce
3/4 cups mozzarella & provolone
cheese
1/4 cup mushrooms
1/4 cup spinach
6 cherry tomatoes

Crust:
1 head cauliflower
1/2 cup shredded mozzarella
1/4 cup grated parmesan
1/2 teaspoon dried oregano
1/2 teaspoon kosher salt
1/4 teaspoon garlic powder
2 eggs, lightly beaten

Prep: 5 minutes

Cook: 11-13 minutes for premade crust/ 30 minutes for crust made from scratch

Total: 18 minutes/ 45 minutes for crust made from scratch

Servings: 4

The first thing you want to do is preheat the oven to 400 degrees so that by the time you're done prepping your crust the oven will be nice and hot for you. I must say this first part is my least favorite part. I've tried to find ways around it, but this is the only way.

Break the cauliflower florets into small pieces, but be careful not to make a mess. I have found cauliflower in strange places because it pops all over the place. This is your warning just in case you decide to go on a breaking spree.

Once the cauliflower florets are broken into small pieces, put them in your food processor until they are finely chopped. You'll want to drain them well once they are processed. I've found that using a paper towel and pressing down will remove all the excess moisture.

In a mixing bowl, add the cauliflower, mozzarella, parmesan, oregano, salt, garlic powder and eggs. Once all your ingredients are mixed together you'll want to put the mixture on your baking sheet and start to form your crust into whatever shape you like. A circle is traditional; however, you can make it into a square, a rectangle, or if you're really fancy, you can make it into a star, which is a favorite with little ones. Now that your crust is formed, bake it for 20 minutes.

I've given you guys my favorite toppings, but you can literally put whatever you like on this pie and you cannot go wrong. Once you've added your toppings to your crust, you want to throw it back in the oven for about 10 minutes or so. As much as I love traditional pizza from my favorite pizza shop, this cauliflower crust is amazing and gets my vote every time. I'm sure you'll feel the same. Enjoy!

Veggie Kabobs

1 teaspoon olive oil

1/2 pound baby potatoes

1/2 teaspoon Mom's Seasoning

1 yellow summer squash

1/2 teaspoon Adobo w/ pepper

1 medium red pepper

1/2 teaspoon garlic powder

5 ounces small portabella mushrooms

Prep: 30 minutes

Cook: 10 minutes

Total: 40 minutes

Servings: 2

*Skewers

First, coat your pan with olive oil and put it on a medium heat. By the time you're done cutting your ingredients, your pan will be hot and ready to simmer. Cut your baby potatoes in half and put them in a quarter of the pan. I used Mom's Seasoning (which can be purchased at www.FromtheHeartCookbook.com), however, if you don't have any, use your favorite seasoning that you use for potatoes, then cover.

Put the potatoes in first and cover them because they take a little longer to cook. You don't want to cook your fresh veggies for very long if you want them to still be semi-crispy. Less heat is also a good way to maintain the nutrients in them. So, we'll add the other ingredients once they are all cut and ready.

Next, you want to cut your summer squash and season with Adobo w/ pepper.

I normally cut mine in slices maybe about the thickness of a 50 page notebook, if that makes sense. You don't want them too thick, yet not so thin that you won't be able to get them on the skewer the way you need them to be. Cut your red pepper into small squares and season with garlic powder. If you look at the picture, you should be able to get an idea of how to cut the peppers, and for the mushrooms, you can leave them whole.

Now it's time to throw the other three ingredients in the pan in their own sections of the pan and add the appropriate seasoning to them. The peppers get the garlic powder and the squash gets the Adobo. Once everything is cooked, uncover and remove from the heat.

I would let it sit for a few minutes so you don't burn your fingers because now is the "fun" part. In no particular order, add the contents of the pan to the skewer.

It's not necessary, but I'm a sauce lover, and when I was done putting everything on the skewers I saw that I had some Tai Sweet Ginger sauce on the door of the fridge and decided to brush some over the kabobs. My, my, my was it DELICIOUS. I hope you guys enjoy them.

Mock Tuna

2 cans garbanzo beans (chickpeas)

3 tablespoons vegan mayo

Dash of salt

A few dashes of pepper

Prep: 10 minutes

Servings: 2

When I first heard about this, I admit I was a little leery because at that point I'd never had chickpeas. When I would see them in the market, the picture on the can never looked appealing, but let me tell you this, you will not be disappointed if you're looking for a good tuna substitute.

When it comes to tuna sandwiches, I prefer mine plain, but please feel free to add any other veggies such as carrots, peppers, onions, etc. Making this is literally identical to making regular tuna. First, you want to drain the water from your chickpeas and put them into a mixing bowl. I prefer to use a potato masher to mash the chickpeas up. Squash them until the peas aren't whole anymore. If you miss a few, it's not that big of a deal. Just make sure the majority are squashed.

Add your mayo to the chickpeas and begin mixing. Then, add your salt and pepper and stir until the seasonings are thoroughly blended into your mixture. Just like that, you're ready for lunch. Add your favorite sandwich toppings and enjoy this lite and healthy lunch.

So delicious!

Crab Soup

18 ounce can cream of mushroom soup
1/4 cup heavy cream
12 ounces claw crab meat
2 teaspoons Old Bay seasoning
salt and pepper (optional)

Prep: 5 minutes

Cook: 20 minutes

Total: 25 minutes

Servings: 4

So... let's talk about this soup. In the process of writing this book, I was tired of market runs and tired of cooking, and I wanted something really quick to make for lunch. I had some tuna left over from the Mockup Tuna and the Avocado Tuna, so I decided to mix the two together so that I would have enough to make a tuna melt. I love soup with sandwiches, but I had no soup.

My wheels started spinning and I had a taste for lobster bisque, but of course I didn't have the ingredients for that. What I did have was some cream of mushroom soup and some crab meat. Why I had heavy cream was beyond me, but I had it and it hadn't expired so it was a go. I legit surprised myself. So I give you guys crab soup.

Pour the cream of mushroom soup into a pot on a low heat. Add the heavy cream, crab meat, Old Bay seasoning and stir. Cover for about 20 minutes. This is a good dish to pair with the Mock Tuna Sandwich. I hope you enjoy it as much as I did.

Salmon Fettuccine

1/2 box fettuccine noodles
Olive oil (1t for noodles, 1T for salmon & 1T to pour over cooked noodles)
1 1/2 pounds fresh Alaskan salmon
2 teaspoons Mom's seasoning (or your favorite seasoning for salmon)
1 pint cherry tomatoes
1 cup fresh spinach
1 teaspoon thyme
1/2 cup blue cheese crumbles

Prep: 10 minutes

Cook: 25 minutes

Total: 35 minutes

Servings: 2

I timed this meal at 25 minutes, but if you cook and prep while the noodles are boiling, it literally takes the length of time it takes the noodles to boil to complete this dish.

With that being said, start to boil your water; I break my noodles in half and drop them into the pot before the water boils. This cuts down on the cook time. Also, put a few drops (approximately one teaspoon) of olive oil in the water so that your noodles don't stick.

When prepping your pans, if possible, use a large enough pan so that you'll be able to put your salmon as well as your tomatoes. If not, two separate pans will do. Pour a tablespoon of olive oil in your pan and put the pan over a medium heat as you start to prep your salmon.

I prefer to take the skin off of my salmon. Rinse your salmon with warm water and pat dry to remove the moisture. Season your salmon evenly on both sides.

While the salmon is cooking up, this is the perfect time to cut your cherry tomatoes in half. Once your salmon starts to get a nice brown color on the bottom, it will be time to flip it to the other side. Flip your salmon and add your tomatoes to the same pan. Just leave a little space in between the tomatoes and the salmon. The idea is for the salmon drippings to give a little flavor to the tomatoes.

After about seven minutes, the salmon, noodles and tomatoes should be thoroughly cooked. Drain your water from the noodles, but leave the noodles in the pot. Take your thyme and sprinkle it in your noodles along with a few drops of olive oil. Stir. Now grab your fresh spinach, tomatoes and blue cheese crumbles and add it to the warm noodles and mix all together.

At this point, your stomach is probably churning due to the aroma and that's a good thing because your meal is complete. Just put your noodle mixture in a plate or bowl of your choice. You can either cut your salmon and mix it in or you can lay it on top of your noodles and veggies. If you want to be fancy, because I know you have more blue cheese crumbles left, you can sprinkle a few more over the top of the finished plate. You will not be disappointed.

A lot of who and what I am is a direct reflection of my mother, Mom-Mom Vette. Growing up, I remember my mom cooking often, but there were always a few meals that stuck with me. The funny part is that some of the meals were what I call "struggle meals."

One of our favorite struggle meals was eggs and rice. I'm definitely not putting an eggs and rice recipe in this book; however, that meal was special to me. As a kid, it showed me creativity and how to make something out of nothing. To date, a lot of the meals I make come from things that are already in the fridge. As much as folks think I enjoy market runs, I don't. I'd rather create from what's already on deck.

Two other meals that stuck with me that my mom used to make were her turkey burgers in the broiler and her onion chicken thighs. It was fascinating to me that she could use an envelope of Lipton Onion Soup mix in two completely different dishes and they would be equally delicious. For years, onion soup mix was my go to, but I learned the hard way that it doesn't go with everything (insert sick emoji face here).

My mom's food was always so flavorful. Whether it was the chicken thighs, the burgers or another one of my favorites, butter noodles with just salt and pepper. Growing up eating those foods taught me the significance of seasoning. My mother showed me that food needs to be evenly seasoned so that each bite is equally as good as the last.

To my favorite Silver Fox, I love you more than words could

A gift for the taste buds!

Mom-Mom Vette's Beyond Turkey Burger

1 teaspoon olive oil

1 pound Beyond Meat

1/2 ounce Lipton Onion Soup Mix
(half of the package)

1/2 cup feta cheese

Prep: 10 minutes

Cook: 20 minutes

Total: 30 minutes

Servings: makes 4
burgers

This is literally the easiest recipe in the book. Coat your pan with olive oil and put it on top of a medium heat. In a mixing bowl, add your Beyond Meat and your Lipton Onion Soup Mix. Then, stir until combined. Now, add the feta to the mix and stir some more.

It's time to shape your patties! This recipe yields four burgers, but if you need more, be sure to double the ingredients. Once the burgers are pattied up, put them in your pan and cover them. Let the first side cook for 7-10 minutes. Then, flip your burgers and cook for the same time on the opposite side.

Just like that, you'll have a burger that's not really a burger, but it will definitely give you the burger vibes you need. You can even try and sneak these in at your next barbeque and your guess won't even know the difference. Enjoy!

This stuffed basa recipe has been one of my favorites for years. It was actually one of the first recipes I put together when I decided to change my diet in 2014. The kicker was, prior to making it, I had no idea of how to stuff a fish. It was challenging because fish is so thin, but I figured it out and it's very simple to do. The goal is to get a taste of both the fish and the filling in every single bite.

Stuffed Basa and Crab Balls

8 ounces lump crabmeat

1 teaspoon Old Bay seasoning

1 teaspoon garlic powder

2 tablespoons whipped veggie cream cheese

1/2 sleeve of Townhouse crackers

2 pieces basa fish (swai)

2 teaspoons Mom's seasoning

1 teaspoon olive oil

Prep: 20 minutes

Cook: 25 minutes

Total: 45 minutes

Servings: 2

First, preheat your oven to 375 degrees. By time you get done prepping, the oven should be ready for you to bake. Put your lump crab meat, old bay, garlic powder and veggie cream cheese in a mixing bowl, and mix thoroughly.

The crackers in this recipe serve as the bread crumbs; I chose Townhouse crackers solely because growing up, Mom (my great grandmother) always had these in the cupboard, so they became my favorite. You can break them up by hand or put them in a bowl and break them with a spoon. Just try and break them down so you don't have big chunks of crackers because you're going to mix this with the crab, seasoning and veggie cream cheese. Once all of these ingredients are mixed together, you can sit the bowl to the side so you can tend to the fish.

Make sure your fish is patted dry. I normally rinse mine and use a few paper towels to get all the moisture out. Now that you've gotten all of the moisture out, use Mom's Seasoning or if you don't have Mom's Seasoning you can use your favorite seasonings just make sure that the fish is seasoned well on both sides. As a reminder, Mom's Seasoning can be purchased at www.FromtheHeartCookbook.com. After you season your fish, it's time to stuff it.

Lay your filets flat. Scoop about two to three teaspoons of filling and spread it on top of the fish evenly. Be sure to leave 1/4 inch of the top and bottom of the fish free of filling. This will make it easier for the next step so you don't make a mess.

Start from the bottom portion of the filet, which is the smallest part of the fish and roll the filet along with the filling all the way to the top. If done properly, it almost resembles a dope seashell.

Coat your baking pan with olive oil so the fish doesn't stick to the pan. Now to prevent your stuffed fish from unraveling you can do one of two things. You can use a toothpick and stick it through the top and the bottom to keep it together or you can lay the fold of the fish along the side of the pan.

With the excess filling, there will be enough to make about 5-7 crab balls, so roll those up and throw them in the pan with the fish. You just want to take them out about 10 minutes before the fish is done because they don't take long to cook. Thank me later!

Enjoy guys!

Honey Glazed Scallops

2 ounces unsalted butter

7 tablespoons honey

1 teaspoon ginger

2 teaspoons soy sauce

1 teaspoon olive oil

1 pound sea scallops

1 teaspoon garlic powder

1 teaspoon black pepper

Prep: 10 minutes

Cook: 20 minutes

Total: 30 minutes

Servings: 2

In a small pot, you'll want to add in your butter, honey, ginger and soy sauce. Simmer on low heat and stir periodically. While your sauce is simmering, coat a saucepan with olive oil and put it on medium heat.

Season one side of your sea scallops with pepper and lay them in your pan pepper side down. Season the other side with garlic powder. You'll want to let the scallops cook for a few minutes on each side, but while you're waiting for them to cook, you can continue to stir and lower on your honey sauce.

When your scallops are done cooking, put them in the honey sauce for about five minutes so the sauce can take to the scallops. While they are in the sauce, take a tablespoon and pour it over parts of the scallops that aren't covered.

Now that your scallops are done, it's time to plate these bad boys. If you want to be fancy and impress your dining guest, pour a little sauce over the scallops and place a few twigs of thyme on top and on the side as seen in the picture. I hope you guys enjoy this one!

A lot of my favorite childhood moments come from a collage of memories that I experienced at my great-grandmother's house. The one thing I remember is that her house was always crowded. She lived in a three story home on 42nd and Parrish Street, in a section of West Philly better known as "Down The Bottom."

At one point in time, my great-grandmother, her sister, my aunt, two of my uncles (who shared a room on the third floor), another uncle and his family of five were at my great-grandmother's house. I was often there on weekends so I was close to all of my family, who for the most part, were siblings of my father. My uncle Chris is my dad's youngest brother. He and I were the closest growing up. Chris and I shared a bond because he was the youngest of the siblings and I was the oldest of the grands, even though we have a little less than a 20 year difference. He has always been my guy and I have always looked up to him.

Chris played a very important part in my life, probably more than he would ever give himself credit. He's the one who taught me how to dribble a basketball, he introduced me to Sugar Ray Leonard, and he is the one solely responsible for my sneaker addiction. Even though he is my uncle, when I was younger he felt more like a big brother. I even addressed him as Chris. The one thing I admired about him is that he always seemed to work, and for the better part of my childhood he worked as a cook. I never knew where, but I knew he cooked.

I remember him coming in with a white or black and white checker uniform that was always stained by sauce and any other residue that managed to splash onto his clothes while preparing food. For some reason, I don't remember him cooking a lot at my great-grandmother's, but when he did, it was always a breakfast sandwich. Trust, these weren't just regular breakfast andwiches. They were perfect breakfast sandwiches, so perfect that hey would taste the exact same way every time. With that, I learned bout consistency while cooking.

onsistency may be the one thing that is most overlooked when it omes to cooking. Often, the food is similar each time a person cooks. may not taste exactly as it did previously, but yet it's edible so the ook is satisfied. Chris introduced me to the concept of being onsistent while cooking and now I take pride in preparing any dish I reate, consistently.

or that, Chris my guy, I appreciate and I love you.

This Wellington recipe is really fun. There is some prep work involved, but it's really easy to make. The first time I made this was back in 2015. It was a special occasion, Mother's Day, and I wanted to make a gourmet meal for my mom.

When I first changed my diet, I would experiment with recipes I'd find on the internet, and I discovered one similar to this one. I wanted to impress my mom and show her that I had been brushing up on my cooking skills. She seemed to enjoy her Wellington and said it was good, but that's what moms are supposed to say (laughing out loud).

The recipe was decent back then, but since that time I've put my spin on it and made it much, much better. This is definitely one for the books!

Seafood Wellington

1 teaspoon olive oil
12 ounces salmon
1/2 pound large shrimp
1 1/2 teaspoon Mom's Seasoning
1 cup fresh spinach
1/2 lemon
Few shakes of pepper
A pinch of sea salt
2 tablespoons veggie cream cheese
Pillsbury Crescent Dough Sheet
1 egg
Splash of almond milk (or whatever milk
you have in your fridge)

Prep: 20 minutes

Cook: 30 minutes

Total: 50 minutes

Servings: 4

The first thing I like to do is coat a pan with one teaspoon of olive oil and put it on top of a low to medium heat. If you have a big enough pan to cook the salmon and the shrimp at the same time, that's perfect. If not, using two separate pans will work as well.

Make sure that your salmon is free of moisture before cooking it. Once you get the moisture out, season one side of the salmon with a half teaspoon of Mom's Seasoning. Put the seasoned side of the salmon in the pan.

While that's starting to cook, you'll want to cut your shrimp in half. When all of the shrimp are cut, throw them in the pan with the salmon and use the rest of your Mom's Seasoning to season the shrimp and the unseasoned side of the salmon. While the seafood is cooking, preheat your oven to 375 degrees.

Take your fresh spinach and put it into a bowl. Squeeze your half lemon ove
the fresh spinach and add a few shakes of pepper along with a pinch or two
of sea salt. Mix together and sit to the side.

Now you can flip your salmon over and remove your shrimp from the pan
Place shrimp into a bowl while waiting for the salmon to finish cooking
Using a spatula, or whatever works for you, start to cut the salmon into smal
pieces once you see that it's about done.

Remove your salmon from the heat so it's not over cooked. You'll be adding
a little more heat to it in the next step. Once the salmon is cut, put it in the
bowl with the shrimp. Due to the warm temperature and the moisture from
the seafood, you may have some drippings in the bowl so make sure you
drain that out before the next step.

Now that the drippings are gone, add your two tablespoons of veggie cream
cheese and mix it in with your seafood. You're almost done, but this is where
it gets a little detailed and you have to take your time.

Open the Pillsbury Crescent sheet. Roll out your cresent on a flat surface, .
use a cutting board for mine. Once it's rolled out, using a knife cut the sheet
down the middle so that you have two identical halves.

Now it's time to grab the spinach mixture you made early on. You want to
make a bed of spinach on top of the crescent sheet, but make sure it's in the
middle of the sheet leaving the edges clean. If done correctly, the crescent
sheet will resemble a picture frame and the spinach would take the place of
the picture. I hope that makes sense.

Next, grab your seafood mixture and spread it on top of the spinach. Don't
worry about using all of it because I want you guys to have a little left over

or a bonus snack. Once you've put your seafood mixture onto the bed of spinach, you'll want to fold the bottom of the crescent sheet upward about a half inch so it covers some of the spinach and the seafood mixture. Repeat that same step for the top of the crescent as well.

Next, grab one side of the crescent sheet and wrap it halfway over the spinach and the mixture. Repeat that step for the last part of the roll, but this time make it overlap the side that you just wrapped. If done correctly, what you see should resemble a burrito.

In a small bowl, crack your eggs. Add your milk and whisk together to make an egg wash. Using a cooking brush, dip the brush into the wash and lightly spread it over your wellington.

After that, you'll want to grease your baking pan or sheet so you're wellington doesn't stick because that would be a disaster after all this work you put in. Carefully pick up your Wellington and put on the baking pan with the side you just brushed face down in the pan. Then, brush the top side of it. Put your Wellington in the oven and let it bake for about 10 minutes or until it browns to your liking.

BONUS SNACK

So, do you remember that leftover seafood mixture?

Add another teaspoon of veggie cream cheese, a pinch of sea salt and a dash of pepper. Refrigerate it for awhile and let it chill. Grab a pack of crackers and I promise your life will never be the same. I hope y'all enjoy this one!

Spicy Shrimp Tacos with Pineapple Slaw

2 cups red cabbage
1 cup shredded carrots
2 tablespoons vegan mayo
3 tablespoons apple cider vinegar
1 1/2 tablespoons lemon juice
1 cup pineapple tidbits
1/4 teaspoon salt
1/2 teaspoon pepper
1 tablespoon olive oil
1 pound colossal shrimp
1/4 teaspoon paprika
1/4 teaspoon chili powder
6 soft tortilla taco shells

Prep: 20 minutes

Cook: 10 minutes

Total: 30 minutes

Servings: 2

Cut your cabbage to your liking. In a mixing bowl, add your cabbage, carrots, vegan mayo, apple cider vinegar, lemon juice, pineapple tidbits, salt and pepper. Mix thoroughly until all the ingredients are evenly combined. I prefer to have my slaw refrigerated before I eat it, but it's not mandatory. Either refrigerate or set aside.

Coat your pan with olive oil and put it on medium heat. Some folks don't peel their shrimp when they cook, but please do so that you can thoroughly enjoy this dish without having to perform surgery before every bite. Cook on one side for about five minutes or until the shrimp begin to brown. Then, flip and do the same on the other side.

The cool taco racks pictured can be purchased from Amazon, and they make it extremely easy to plate this dish. However, if you don't have the rack, you can simply lay the soft tortilla shells on a plate and rest one taco on the next.

To fill your taco, line the bottom of the soft taco shell with your slaw. Top it with the perfectly seasoned colossal shrimp. I promise you, "Taco Tuesday" will never be the same. Enjoy!

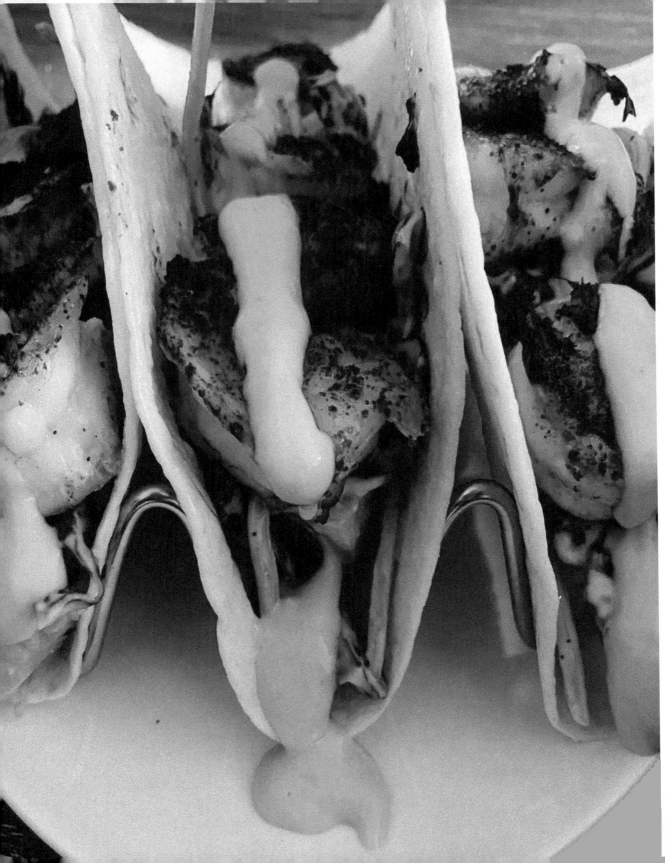

This is a fun colorful recipe and is also good for your little ones; the one who won't eat traditionally prepared veggies. Just tell them they'r "fun cakes" or something creative and they'll eat them up.

The good thing about this dish is that there are multiple ways to prepar it. You can really use whatever combination of veggies you like. Jus season them well and you cannot lose. I prefer to use broccoli, corn and carrots for mine.

Veggie Cakes

2 cups fresh cut broccoli

3/4 cup shredded carrots

1 cup canned corn

1/2 cup sweet onion

3 large eggs

1 cup seasoned bread crumbs

2 teaspoons garlic powder

1 tablespoon olive oil

Prep: 15 minutes

Cook: 20 minutes

Total: 35 minutes

Servings: 3

Remove the florets of broccoli from the stalk and cut them into small bite-size pieces. I use shredded carrots, but I still cut them in half. Drain your cup of corn as much as possible. Then, dice your sweet onion.

Once everything is cut, place into a mixing bowl. Add your eggs, seasoned bread crumbs and garlic powder to the mixing bowl as well. Stir until all ingredients are combined.

Now, using three or four tablespoons at a time, begin to form your veggie cakes. I prefer my cakes to be large; however, if you prefer a smaller size, I recommend using two tablespoons per cake.

Coat your pan with olive oil and place your cakes in the pan on a medium heat. After about 10 minutes or so (5-7 minutes for smaller cakes), flip your cakes and cook for the same amount of time on the opposite side. I hope you guys enjoy it!

Salmon Lo Mein

1/2 pack lo mein noodles (10 ounce package)
1 teaspoon olive oil
1pound salmon
1 teaspoon garlic powder
1 teaspoon Adobo
1/2 pound snow peas
8 ounces mushrooms
1/2 cup Thai chili sauce
2 teaspoons soy sauce
salt and pepper (optional)

Prep: 10 minutes

Cook: 20 minutes

Total: 30 minutes

Servings: 4

First, you'll want to boil your noodles in a large pot so that they can be finished close to the same time as your salmon. This way, everything can be served together and everything will be hot. (Use instructions from the package to determine how much water is needed.) I typically use about half of a box of noodles, and break them in half so they aren't super long.

Grab your large saucepan and coat it with olive oil. Then, sit it on medium heat. Use your garlic powder and Adobo to season your salmon. Let your salmon cook on one side for about seven minutes. You should have a nice brown color and a slight crust, which means it's time to flip the salmon over to the other side. While the second side is cooking, use a spatula to break your salmon into smaller pieces.

Now, add your snow peas and mushrooms to the pan with your salmon. Cover and turn the heat down low. In a cup, mix your soy sauce and Thai chili sauce well. Then, pour the mixture into the pan with the salmon, peas and mushrooms. It's optional to top this dish off with a little salt and pepper.

By now, your noodles should be done and it's safe to drain the water from them by using a strainer. Please use pot holders because the pot will be hot. Now it's time to eat. Take a few tongs full of noodles, put them in your favorite bowl or plate and top them with your salmon mixture. Like many of these dishes, this one has become a new favorite of mine. I hope you guys enjoy it!

Fried Sprouts

1 cup whole wheat flour
1 teaspoon chili powder
1 teaspoon garlic powder
1/2 teaspoon pepper
10 ounces fresh brussel sprouts
2 tablespoons peanut oil
1/2 red onions (cut into rings)
1/2 cup jalapeño peppers
Dash of salt optional

Prep: 15 minutes

Cook: 10 minutes

Total: 25 minutes

Servings: 2

*Air fryer preferred

Add flour and all of the seasonings into a bag. Shake it well, so that all the seasonings can be evenly distributed. Next, you'll want to set your air fryer to 390 degrees for ten minutes. Now it's time to slice your brussel sprouts in half and set them to the side. Grab your red onion and cut it in half, once it's cut in half be careful and slice your red onion into rings so you have the onion ring effect, and set them to the side as well.

Brush your peanut oil on all of the brussel sprouts. Once they are all coated, drop them in your bag with your flour mixture. So you don't make a mess, grab a pair of tongs to take the sprouts out of the flour and slightly shake the excess flour off.

By now the fryer should be nice and hot and you can put the brussels in. If your air fryer is like mine, halfway through it will tell you to flip your food. If not, at five minutes open your fryer, shake the brussels around a little and add your red onions.

When your fryer has two minutes left, throw your jalapeños and let the time run out. Check your fridge because I'm sure you have some of your favorite dipping sauces on the door, pour in a dipping bowl and enjoy this delicious appetizer.

The love I have for potatoes is unreal. I literally can eat them in any form. However, I have a strange love-hate relationship with potato salad. There is just something about the eggs that doesn't always sit right with me. So with that being said ladies and gents, boys and girls, let me introduce you to this Roasted Potato Salad.

Roasted Potato Salad

4 medium-sized Idaho potatoes
1 tablespoon olive oil
1 teaspoon Mom's Seasoning
2 large avocados
1 tablespoon vegan mayo
1/4 teaspoon pink Himalayan salt
(optional)
1/2 teaspoon paprika

Prep: 10 minutes

Cook: 25 minutes

Total: 35 minutes

Servings: 2

Tip: Refrigerate before serving

The best way to make this dish is to peel the potatoes first. Normally, I don't, but for this dish to get the nice light green color from the avocado, peeling them is a must. Once the potatoes are peeled, cut them into small cubes. Put one tablespoon of olive oil into your non-stick pan. Take a paper towel and spread the oil around the pan so your potatoes don't stick.

Put your potatoes in the pan and evenly distribute your teaspoon of Mom's Seasoning all over them. Cover and let them cook for about 20 minutes on medium heat.

While the potatoes are cooking, cut your avocados with a sharp knife in the middle all the way around and take out the core. Using a spoon, scoop out the avocado and put it into a small bowl.

Mash the avocado until all the chunks are gone, then add your vegan mayo. Mix the two together.

By this time, your potatoes should be almost finished. You can use a fork to poke through the potatoes. If the fork goes straight through easily, then you are good to go. Once the potatoes are done, remove them from the pan, preferably with a set of tongs or something equivalent, so that you don't transfer the excess oil from the pan into your bowl. Let sit for about five minutes before you add your avocado/mayo mixture.

Mix the avocado/mayo mixture in with your potatoes. Once mixed, you can add a very small amount of salt if you choose. I prefer pink Himalayan, but just a little for taste, and then top with paprika.

I know at this point the salad smells delicious, but put it in the fridge for a few so it can cool. I promise you won't be disappointed. I hope you guys enjoy this one. It's one of my favorites.

Beyond Sketti

1 teaspoon olive oil
1/2 box veggie pasta noodles
2 Beyond Sausage links
1 teaspoon olive oil
1/4 cup red onions
1/4 cup green peppers
1 teaspoon minced garlic
1 1/2 teaspoons garlic powder
1 can diced tomatoes
1/2 cup tomato sauce
1/4 cup vodka sauce
Dash of salt
Dash of pepper

Prep: 10 minutes

Cook: 20 minutes

Total: 30 minutes

Servings: 4

Before we fire up the air fryer, put a teaspoon of olive oil in a pot with water on medium heat and add a half box of veggie pasta noodles. The water should cover the noodles completely. Now crack out your air fryer and throw two Beyond Sausage links in for five minutes. Once your Beyond Sausages are done, sit them to the side.

Coat a large saucepan with olive oil. Add your onions, peppers, minced garlic and garlic powder to the saucepan and sauté. Once it has a nice sizzle, add your diced tomatoes, tomato sauce and vodka sauce to the pan, turn your heat down a little. Stir, then cover.

While the contents in the pan are simmering, slice up your Beyond Sausage and add them to the pot. Keep covered, but remove from heat.

After the noodles have boiled, drain them to remove all of the water. At this point you can go one of two ways. You can add your noodles to the sauce and mix it altogether, or if you're like me, place the noodles in your favorite bowl and pour your sauce over top. Sprinkle some fresh parmesan cheese and enjoy!

My love for cooking came directly from my childhood best friend, Willie Mae Smith, also known as Mom. Willie Mae just so happened to be my Great GrandMother on my father's side. I never had the opportunity to meet my father's mother due to her passing before I was born. However, I was blessed to have Willie Mae. She definitely filled that void and kept me close to her.

Like most of our elders, especially ones from the south, Mom was known for her cooking. Her specialty was her golden fried chicken, which was always cooked to perfection. She never made a bad batch. As delicious as her chicken was, it wasn't the chicken that intrigued me. It was the effort that she put into the small things which made every meal a big deal.

The first time I was introduced to plating was in Willie Mae's kitchen in the late 80's. I would be lying if I said I could remember the exact day because that was what she did on a regular basis. I vividly remember Saturday afternoon lunches being routinely served.

The way this woman would plate something as simple as cold cuts for afternoon sandwiches was a presentation that I remember like no other. The bread was perfectly stacked. The tomatoes were fire red, evenly cut and spread across a white saucer. The cold cuts were individually rolled and there were always a variety of cheeses and sandwich spreads. The lemonade was always cold and it was served in the perfect pitcher, which seemed to make it that much colder.

At a young age, it was easy to understand why her food looked so good and smelled good too. It was the love that was put into every dish. Mom understood the concept of family. She was the backbone that kept us all together. For that, and for giving me a piece of her

Mexican food has always been a favorite of mine, even when I was younger and thought that Taco Bell was considered Mexican food. To my young surprise, it wasn't. As I grew older, traditional mexican food has never failed me and burritos have always been my favorite.

I used to prefer chicken or even a healthy steak burrito. Since I no longer eat meat and I'm not fond of all meat substitutes, I had to find something that I thought would still be filling and savory, so I decided to go with the sweet potato and black bean burrito.

Using black beans was new to me. Previously, I would have asked to have them left out of my burrito, but over the years I've grown to like them. Mixing the beans with the sweet potatoes gives the perfect mix of sweet and savory at the same time.

Sweet Potato & Black Bean Burrito

2 ounces vegan butter

2 small sweet potatoes

1 tablespoon brown sugar

1/2 cup diced red onions

1 pouch 90-seconds rice with cilantro

2 cans seasoned black beans

1 teaspoon garlic powder

4 soft tortilla wraps

Prep: 10 minutes

Cook: 20 minutes

Total: 30 minutes

Servings: 4

To start, put your vegan butter in a large saucepan on medium heat. While the pan is warming, cut your sweet potatoes into small cubes and put them in the sauce pan. Take you brown sugar and sprinkle it over the potatoes. Then, cover the potatoes so that they can cook properly.

While the potatoes are cooking, dice up your onion, and let me tell y'all about this 90-seconds rice. For a lot of people, rice isn't the easiest to make, and even for me, it took quite some time to perfect it. I'm not the biggest fan of the microwave, but trust when I tell you, you wouldn't know it was microwaved unless you saw it come out of the microwave.

There is a name brand one that I used to use; however, I tripped over another pouch in the international aisle at the grocery store. It has cilantro in it and it's amazing! With that being said, throw your 90-seconds rice in the microwave and don't forget to tear two small slits in both sides of the bag at the top because if you don't the rice will remind you that you didn't when you hear the loud pop. I'm telling y'all this from experience.

By this time, the potatoes should be about done. To make sure, take a fork and if it goes straight through the potatoes you are good to go. If so, turn the heat down to low.

Open and drain the water from your can of black beans and add them to the saucepan with the potatoes. Add the rice and onions too. Stir until mixed well. Season with your garlic powder and let simmer for about five minutes. I recommend mixing everything together so when it's in the burrito you get to taste all the ingredients in every bite.

Now that all of your ingredients are cooked, go to YouTube and search how to wrap a burrito, unless you've worked at Chipotle and you're a pro. I'm no pro, so I definitely used YouTube.

Cheat
DAY

The one misconception that folks have about changing your diet is thinking that you cannot have sweets or desserts. Welp, they're wrong because you can. These Oatmeal Craisin Cookies are delicious, and like everything else we've been cooking so far, they don't take very long to prepare.

Growing up, I wasn't the biggest sweets eater, but I would always appreciate a good cookie. I remember going down to the Gallery, and after a day of browsing the mall, I would always make sure I had a few bucks to grab some warm cookies from the food court for the el (train) ride home. Chocolate chip and oatmeal raisin were always my favorites. I can taste them as I'm writing.

Oatmeal Craisin Cookies

1 teaspoon baking powder

1 teaspoon baking soda

1 1/2 cups wheat flour

1 1/2 cups old fashioned oats

1/4 cup almond milk

1/2 cup brown sugar

1/2 cup honey

1/2 cup vegan butter (softened)

1/3 cup dried cranberries

Coconut oil spray

Prep: 15 minutes

Cook: 15 minutes

Total: 30 minutes

Servings: 10 large cookies

For this recipe, it's easier and less of a mess if you use two bowls, but first preheat your oven to 350 degrees. In one bowl, you'll want to mix all of your dry ingredients. Add your baking powder, baking soda, flour and oats to the first bowl and mix them all together.

Now in your second bowl you'll want to combine your milk, sugar and honey. Melt your butter. Let it cool for a few minutes. Once the butter is cool, add the butter to the other liquid ingredients.

Little by little, add the contents of the dry mixture to the bowl of liquid ingredients and stir. Once all ingredients from both bowls are combined, the mixture will start to become slightly dough-like. That is when you should add your dried cranberries and mix them in as well.

Now the fun part, coat your cookie sheet or baking pan so the cookies don't stick. For this, I use coconut oil spray on my cookie sheet. I feel as though you can't make a cookie too big or too small but I prefer my cookies to be rather large. I used a tablespoon to scoop out the dough and made them into balls about the size of golf balls and placed them on the sheet making sure that they were not touching.

Once you have all your cookies on the sheet place them in the oven and let them bake for about 10 minutes. Just make sure to continuously check them if you're not an expert baker, so that you don't burn the bottom. I'm giving this advice from personal experience. I hope you guys enjoy them.

First let me say, I LOVE CORNBREAD. When I was younger, like younger -younger, I remember my great grandmother used to always make fresh cornbread and she would give me a cup of buttermilk. For some odd reason, I would put the bread in the milk and eat it with a spoon. I probably couldn't do that now without losing my lunch, but I do remember how good the cornbread would taste. I know for a fact that I could never duplicate her amazing recipe, but this one isn't bad at all, and it almost tastes like cake if you do it right. Once you start making things from scratch there is really no going back to boxed goods. It's addictive.

Strawberry Cornbread

2 large eggs
1/4 cup butter (melted)
1/2 cup milk
1/2 cup half & half
1/4 cup honey
1 cup whole wheat flour
1 cup cornmeal
1/4 cup sugar
1/2 teaspoon salt
1 tablespoon baking powder
1 1/2 cups fresh sliced strawberries

Prep: 20 minutes

Cook: 30 minutes

Total: 50 minutes

Servings: 8

The first thing you'll want to do is preheat your oven to 400 degrees. Grab a mixing bowl and mix all of your liquid ingredients together. Don't forget to beat your two eggs before adding them with your milk, half and half, honey and melted butter. Make sure the butter is room temperature before adding. Once everything is added, mix it together and sit it to the side.

Now grab another mixing bowl and add all of your dry ingredients (flour, cornmeal, sugar, salt and baking powder). Then, mix them together. Now that you have the ingredients of both bowls mixed up, slowly add your dry ingredients to the liquid ingredients, adding approximately 1/4 cup at a time. Stir until combined.

Now you can add your sliced strawberries and mix them in as well.

Once everything is mixed up, wash your hands, grab a clean spoon and taste the batter because it will be delicious.

Here is the trick to making this cornbread turn out to be amazing. Grab a pat of butter and coat your castor iron pan. Once the pan is coated, add your batter to the pan. Turn on the oven light so you can watch and enjoy the amazing aroma that will come from your oven. I hope you guys enjoy this one. It's one of my favorites.

One of my favorite breakfast dishes my mom used to make when we lived in our 2 bedroom apartment on North 63rd Street was fried apples. I don't really remember having them with anything else, but those apples alone were amazing.

This dish is super simple and can be used in a variety of ways. You can eat this fruit salad alone, you can add some nonfat yogurt to it or you can have it over a bowl of ice cream.

Sautèed Fruit Salad with Walnuts

1 ounce butter

2 red apples

2 pears

2 peachees

1/4 teaspoon nutmeg

1 teaspoon cinnamon

1 teaspoon brown sugar

¾ cup walnuts

Prep: 5 minutes

Cook: 10 minutes

Total: 15 minutes

Servings: 2

Take your ounce of butter and add it to your saucepan. Then, set it on medium heat. While your pan is warming, slice your apples, pears, and peaches and toss them in the pan. Sprinkle your nutmeg, your cinnamon and your brown sugar on top of your fruit. Cover and let it simmer for about 10 minutes.

Periodically, using a mixing spoon, uncover and mix the fruit around so that it doesn't stick to the pan when the fruit is almost done. Throw in your walnuts and in a few minutes your kitchen will smell amazing and you will have a healthy dessert that you can eat one of three ways. Enjoy!

was always dope to me that my mom and her sisters have always been close, so close that when I was younger we all pretty much lived within walking distance from one another. Two of my aunts have children and all of us are very close in age so coming up my cousins were my friends and I spent a lot of time over their houses. I have one aunt whose house I was over more often than the others, Aunt Gina, my mom's oldest sister.

Aunt Gina is one of the nicest and coolest people you'll ever meet. However, when we were younger, I didn't see it that way. My aunt always demanded and required respect. She would show love, but she would also discipline and if she said something she meant it. Growing up, I was a real picky eater and I was raised in the era that if it was prepared for you, you would eat it.

When I was young my aunt had a daycare and being as though I didn't go to kindergarten, I was often in the mix with the daycare kids. I don't blame her for her cooking methods. She made meals in bulk and did not cater to my picky needs. However, I HATED peanut butter and jelly sandwiches. They were just a thing that I could never understand.

Now, as a kid I thought, better yet I knew I was smarter than everybody. While that was never really the case, I would still push the envelope with my aunt. Lunch time at the daycare was like clockwork. It happened at noon daily. Most of her lunches were my favorite, but PB&J day was a day that I would rather run from. Days that my aunt would give me these PB&J sandwiches I would attempt to outthink her and make her think I was eating them when we all knew that I wasn't.

I would wait until lunch was served and give her time to become occupied with some of the other kids. I would sneak Into the shed kitchen and launch my sandwich over the top of the fridge with hopes of it never being found again. Granted, I was only about 5 or 6 at the time, but sandwich after sandwich after sandwich, I would launch these jawns over the top of the fridge. One day my aunt decided to clean behind the fridge and to her surprise she discovered my PB&J collection. I'm pretty sure she was livid! Ironically, as an adult I love peanut butter so much that I can eat it out the jar with a spoon

Aunt Gina, I love you and because of our funny story I wanted to name this

Aunt Gina's PB&J Smoothie

1/2 cup blueberries

4 strawberries

1/2 banana

2 tablespoons peanut butter

1/2 cup almond milk

1 tablespoon honey

Prep: 5 minutes

Servings: 1

Simply add all ingredients into your favorite smoothie maker and blend.

Cora "Maxine" Taylor was my mother's mom, my grandmother. M
grandmother was just one of those people you couldn't help but love and si
loved to cook. She cooked so much. It was to the point that cooking seeme
like her job. As I got older, I realized why, but I'll address that at the end of thi
passage. My grandmother was known for cooking a handful of things, fror
her fried chicken to her mac and cheese, and all the way down to her swee
potato pies.

Being young and sitting in this small sweatbox-like kitchen watching he
cook is where I was introduced to castor iron pots and pans. This one pc
and pan set in particular put in so much work over the years they becam
discolored, but the discoloration had no effect on the taste or the quality c
the food. It always came out better than you expected it to be. I'm blesse
that my grandmother and grandfather had 5 children, one uncle wa
deceased before I came along. They all had children who, to this day, ar
more like siblings than cousins.

I never thought our family was super big, but the size was just right for me
and for my grandmother for that sake. Often on holidays, Grandmother'
apartment was the meetup spot. How all of us fit into this two bec
apartment is beyond me, but we made it work.

The adults sat on the couch and loveseat and the kids all found a spc
somewhere on the floor with news paper or a magazine under our plates "s
that we wouldn't make a mess". The one thing that always stood out to m
over my cousins and me bickering, was the sound of my mom and her
siblings laughing and talking over the tv.

On the far right side of the couch, would be my Grandmother sitting i
a nylon sweatsuit with a turtleneck to match, with her legs crossed, sipping
her iced tea out of a tall bronze color glass. She would be exhausted fror
cooking so much to the point she wouldn't even eat, but she would sit there
with a look of satisfaction on her face because she was able to feed the folk
that she loved. That's when I realized what cooking was all about.

It's about making people happy. In particular, your loved ones. M
Grandmother took pride in that, and because of you Cora "Maxine" Taylor,
was able to create "From The Heart." I'm pretty sure I speak for all of us, Fror
Aunt Gina all the way down to Tenisha, when I say we miss you, we love yo

CPSIA information can be obtained
at www.ICGtesting.com
Printed in the USA
BVHW021528110221
599918BV00007BA/17